Feeling angry is
normal and doesn't mean
you are doing something wrong,
but it is important to know what
to do when this big feeling comes
along.

WHAT'S INSIDE

#1

What does anger feel like?

When you know how anger feels for you it can act like an ALARM...

...to remind you that you need to take control and work on feeling calm.

Recognising anger is the first step to managing it.

Anger can make your breathing fast and your heartbeat start to race.

It can make you feel really tense and put a frown upon your face.

It can make your head feel sore or give you a stomach ache.

It can make you feel all dizzy, you may even start to shake.

Anger can make your tummy do all sorts of strange things. You might feel sick, get butterflies or need to poo.

You might begin to clench your teeth on the way to anger mode...

...or suddenly get really hot and feel ready to explode.

You may even get so hot you start to sweat.

It can make you want to
scream or shout,
and say things you wouldn't
normally say.

You are loved no matter
what but some behaviours
are not okay.

Shouting might
feel good when
you're angry, but
it may scare those
around you.

Anger can also have
a big impact on your mind.

You might feel sad and
grumpy and have a hard
time being
kind.

Anger can make it
hard to feel relaxed,
you may feel
irritated and start
to dislike the people
you're with or the
situation you are in.

Remember: Anger feels different for everyone, notice how it feels for you.

Feel it and observe it, never ignore it. Recognising your anger alarm gives you the chance to think before you react.

If you don't notice your anger alarm going off, you could express your anger in unhelpful ways, such as:

Saying hurtful things

Hitting or pinching

Breaking things

Threatening people

Kicking

Spitting

Pushing people

Throwing things

Slamming doors

Yelling

You may experience some behaviours that are not listed, everyone reacts differently when angry.

The next chapter will give you some helpful and safe ways to deal with your anger instead.

#2

How can I manage my anger?

If you let your anger stay, relationships could be damaged...

...so let's learn some different ways that anger can be managed.

Remember, anger is not the problem. You just need to make sure you respond to it in helpful ways.

There are lots of different ways to control anger, you need to find what works for you.

It might take some time and practice but keep going until you do.

Repeat this 3 times:
"I won't give up. It may take time to learn how to control my anger."

Breathing in for 3 counts and out for 4, a few times in a row...

...can really help to calm you down and let your anger go.

Tip: Close your eyes and focus on every breath, notice your lungs fill up and empty again.

Explaining why you are feeling angry can help it disappear.

It's easier to solve a problem if you use your words to make it clear.

Writing down how you're feeling can help to clear your mind.

When you're calm a solution is much easier to find.

Using a journal will help you explore your emotions.

$P = r^2 \pi$
$\Delta t = T - \frac{3a}{x}$
$\tan(2a) = \frac{\tan(a)}{\tan^2(a)}$
$\sin \beta$
$\pi \approx 3,1415$
$h = \sqrt{a \times b}$
$x_{1/2} = \frac{b \pm (a-c)}{\sqrt{2a}}$
$x = 4 - 3y^2$
$S = \int 5t\,dt$

It's good to take some space if you feel like you might be mean.

You could talk to someone you trust and solve the problem as a team.

Where can you go to get some space and calm down?

If you find that when you're angry, you want to scream and shout...

...move away and find a different tactic to let your anger out.

High energy exercises like jumping jacks or running can help burn off your angry energy.

Challenge:
Try and paint or draw your anger.

You could try to distract yourself by doing something you enjoy.

Perhaps watching your favourite programme or playing with your toys.

Do you have a favourite toy?

If you're stuck in an angry place and feeling full of hate.

A powerful way to feel peaceful again is to sit and meditate.

Meditation takes practice and it might feel weird to start with! You can find lots of kids meditation videos on YouTube.

Try thinking of something you love when you are in an angry place.

Perhaps a person or a song that puts a smile upon your face.

Laughing is also a fantastic way to get rid of anger. Watch a funny video or read some jokes.

Feeling loved can get rid of anger, try cuddling someone tight.

It feels much better to be kind and have fun than being in a fight.

Repeat this 3 times:
"Even when I am angry, I can still be kind."

If you feel like you are stuck inside your anger zone...

...ask someone to help you, don't go through it alone.

Here are some more things you could try to help you to calm down and control your anger:

Give yourself a hug

Play with sand or slime

Squish playdough

Read a book

Blow into your hands

Count backwards from 10

Jump or jog on spot

Bounce on a trampoline

Push a wall as hard as you can

Drink cold water

Say something kind to yourself

Do something funny, throw anger away.

Put a cold flannel
on your forehead

Smile

Squeeze a
squishy toy.

Close your eyes and think
of your favourite place

Shake a
calm down jar

Roar like
a lion

Sing the
alphabet

Put your hands
in your pockets

Yoga

Watch
a film

Write a letter
or a story

Kick a ball
outside

Dance

#3

Why do
I
feel angry?

Whatever your reason there isn't one that's too small.

There is no right or wrong reason for feeling angry, everyone's unique.

Everyone has different things that can make their anger peak.

Some common reasons are: Feeling unheard, misunderstood, or not getting what you want.

No one else has had the
same life as you,
so what makes you feel
angry will be different too.

Everyone has different
things to worry about, and
different things that make
their anger come out.

Sometimes you might feel angry instead of how you're really feeling inside...

...getting angry can feel better than dealing with the feelings it's trying to hide.

When a situation makes you sad you might get angry first.

Focus on how you were feeling before anger came about.

If you find the reason behind it, it will be much easier to sort out.

Have you ever felt angry because you thought you were being left out?

If you have things going on in your life making you feel sad...

...you might find a lot more situations start making you feel mad.

Upsetting memories from your past can also be a trigger...

...it can help to talk to a grown-up you trust and work through these together.

Who can you talk to?

A parent?
A relative?
A teacher?

Challenge:
Complete a yoga for
kids video.
Yoga is a great
calming form of
exercise!

Staying fit and active can stop anger coming your way.

So try to get your body moving at some point in your day.

Do you have a favourite sport you like to watch or play?

Feeling hungry or tired
can also trigger anger,
so be sure to treat
yourself kind!

If you eat well, sleep well
and exercise.
You'll have a much more
positive mind.

What could be hiding behind your anger?

It can be helpful to think of anger like a mask to other feelings you may be having. It can disguise...

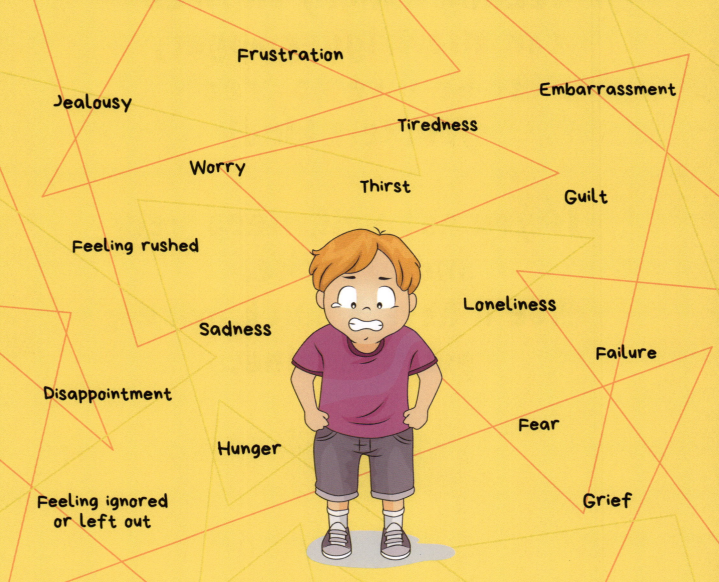

Frustration

Jealousy

Embarrassment

Tiredness

Worry

Thirst

Guilt

Feeling rushed

Loneliness

Sadness

Failure

Disappointment

Fear

Hunger

Feeling ignored
or left out

Grief

#4

Do I need to make things right?

When you hurt someone
(even if you didn't mean to)...

...saying sorry is hard,
but it's the right thing
to do.

An apology doesn't
always need to
be spoken. It can
be a smile, a big
hug, or an act of
kindness.

Remember anger is a
normal emotion,
it is okay to be angry.
Apologise only for any
unacceptable actions
you took because
of it.

Show yourself
love and kindness
if you do something
wrong.

Fix it if you can, let it go
and then move
on.

You might need to
tidy up toys
you've thrown or
wait for your
turn in a game.

Try not to take
other peoples actions
personally.

Choose to
forgive and forget
and let your anger go
free.

So even if someone was really unkind to you...

...don't hold onto your anger it's not healthy to do.

You deserve to be treated with kindness. If someone isn't being nice to you, you don't have to play with them, & don't forget you can ask a grown-up for help.

Taking control of your anger will take practice, but you are stronger than you know!

Keep using what you have learnt from this book and soon you'll be a pro.

This book is presented solely for advice and entertainment purposes. The information provided is designed to provide helpful information on the subject discussed.

The content is the sole expression and opinion of its authors, You are responsible for your own choices, actions, and results.

We advise you to contact a medical professional if you are struggling with any anger related difficulties with your child.

Printed in Great Britain
by Amazon